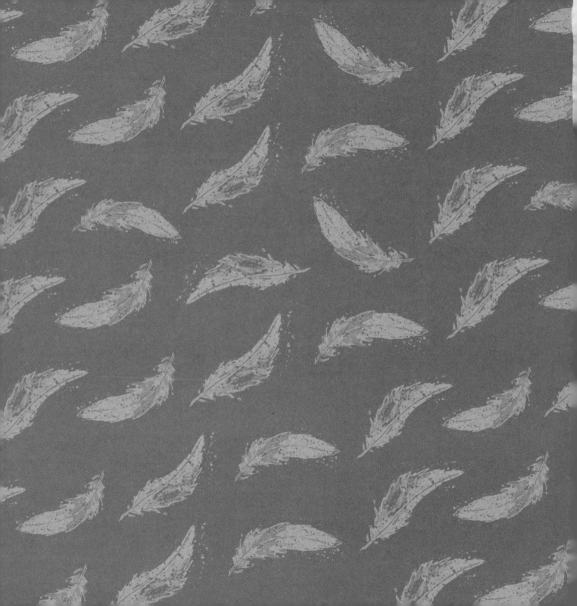

WILD WISDOM

ANIMAL STORIES OF THE SOUTHWEST

By Rae Ann Kumelos ¤ With artwork by Jan Taylor

Rio Nuevo Publishers®
P. O. Box 5250
Tucson, AZ 85703-0250
(520) 623-9558, www.rionuevo.com

Library of Congress Cataloging-in-Publication Data

Names: Kumelos, Rae Ann, 1958– author. | Taylor, Jan, 1960– illustrator.
Title: Wild wisdom : animal stories of the southwest / by Rae Ann Kumelos ;
    artwork by Jan Taylor.
Description: Tucson, AZ : Rio Nuevo Publishers, 2016.
Identifiers: LCCN 2016011798 | ISBN 9781940322100 (hardcover) | ISBN 1940322103 (hardcover)
Subjects: LCSH: Indians of North America–Southwest, New–Folklore. | Animals–Folklore.
Classification: LCC E78.S7 K84 2016 | DDC 398.24/50979–dc23
LC record available at https://lccn.loc.gov/2016011798

Managing Editor: Aaron Downey
Book design: Katie Jennings Campbell

Printed in China.

10 9 8 7 6 5 4 3 2

With thanks to all of my animal friends,
especially the Kitties.
For Mom and Dad,
with love and gratitude.

−R.A.K.

To all the animals, wild or not,
that have magically touched my life!

−J.T.

n n n

CONTENTS

INTRODUCTION

¤ ¤ ¤

History may give us the facts and figures of a moment in time, but myth tells us about the spirit and soul of the time. Twentieth-century songwriter Stephen Schwartz perfectly captures the spirit of the Native American concept of timeless harmony and unity with nature in these lyrics: *The rainstorm and the river are my brothers / The heron and the otter are my friends / And we are all connected to each other / In a circle, in a hoop that never ends.* Expressed in written and oral traditions from countless cultures, this sentiment of animal wisdom and connection has been a vital element of stories shared around the world for centuries.

But why is Native American tradition the standard for this timeless connection to the natural world? Because Native stories speak from a living, relevant belief system and tradition that has resonated for thousands of years, and that tribal cultures consider to be true.

Dennis Tedlock, an authority on Zuni culture, says these true Native stories are called a *chimiky'ana'kowa*. Paul Zolbrod, a scholar of Navajo literary tradition, describes a *chimiky'ana'kowa* story as belonging to a "period when the world was 'soft' and easily shaped and reshaped. The events it tells account for the way things are." Because the stories are believed to be true, they have a tremendous influence on tribal people and how they interact with the animals and the world around them. Franc Johnson Newcomb, who along with her husband ran a trading post on the Navajo reservation for many years, became a renowned expert on Navajo culture, and illustrates the effect of the stories on daily life: because so many birds are considered holy, the "Navajo reservation is considered a veritable bird sanctuary." You will see exactly why Turkey is *still* considered holy when you meet him in "Turkey Saves Thanksgiving for Everyone but Himself."

The stories we tell about animals both determine and reflect our relationship with them. Perhaps Native stories resonate because they do not follow the established paradigm of animals as commodities, tools, and resources simply for our use. Instead, the stories convey appreciation of the animal not as an object but as a valued presence. And Native folklore has communicated for centuries what modern-day study is beginning to prove: animals play a crucial role in inspiring and guiding human beings to embrace our own better natures, in addition to warning what will happen if we indulge our lesser natures. In "A Dazzling Display of Cosmic Disarray," this is especially true for Coyote, who consistently shows us what *not* to do, by doing it.

For the non-Native reader, it is sometimes unclear whether the divine animal-people in the stories are actually people, animals, people dressed as animals, or animals dressed as people. In the tribal stories, the boundaries between human and animal are fluid and permeable. Karl Luckert, an authority on tribal spiritual culture, explains that in pre-human mythical times, all living beings existed in a state of flux: their external forms were interchangeable. This state of flux is where the oral traditions of tribal culture developed. However, when the Native creation events occurred and the People emerged into our present world, what most Navajo call the Fifth World, the flux ended, and, Luckert explains, people fixed "permanently—at least in the realm where ordinary mortal men now live—to particular types of garments, shapes and sizes." Humans and non-humans chose permanently whatever "costume" they wished to wear. That is why Hummingbird is still wearing his "costume" in "Hummingbird's Healing Harmony"; as a Holy One he just preferred to remain a hummingbird.

Joseph Campbell suggests that for non-Native people, the fairy tales and stories known best "are of Europe, not of our adopted continent." Yet by reading the Native stories, he adds, perhaps it's "possible that the powers of the continent are at work on us . . . and in us." The animals featured in this book are most often associated with the Southwest and California, and have a special connection to the air, light, desert, streams, ocean, mountains, and canyons that form this beautiful part of the country. They invite us to reflect on how our own stories and interactions with animals might be better honored.

Our selections are gathered from three main sources: ethnographers of the nineteenth and twentieth centuries who were dedicated to recording and preserving the stories from various tribes, modern-day Native storytellers whose meticulous retelling of their own and other traditions keep them relevant and accessible, and dedicated scholars who study the Native stories as a rich oral and literary tradition of the Americas. In retelling these stories, we have remained true to the original accounts but have refreshed and embellished them a bit, to introduce or reawaken them for today's audience.

Religious scholar Christine Downing believes that "myths about a golden age are about a longed-for future." The longed-for future is here in the form of these stories. Through the gift of ethnographers, scholars, and native storytellers, we invite you to enter the circle as you wish, and with the help and wisdom of the animals, find your own connection to the timeless hoop that never ends.

¤ ¤ ¤
BIBLIOGRAPHY

Downing, Christine. *Mythologies of the Monotheistic Traditions*. Pacifica Graduate Institute. Carpinteria, California, 2003.

King, Jeff, Maud Oakes, and Joseph Campbell. *Where The Two Came To Their Father: A Navajo War Ceremonial Given by Jeff King*. 1943. Bollingen Series I. Princeton: Princeton University Press, 1991.

Luckert, Karl W. *The Navajo Hunter Tradition*. Tucson: University of Arizona Press, 1975.

Newcomb, Franc Johnson. *Navajo Omens and Taboos*. Santa Fe: Rydal, 1940.

Schwartz, Stephen. "Colors of the Wind." *Pocahontas*. Burbank, CA: Walt Disney Home Entertainment, 2000.

Zolbrod, Paul. *Reading the Voice: Native American Oral Poetry on the Written Page*. Salt Lake City: University of Utah Press, 1995.

Owl

DAY AND NIGHT: YOU CAN BET ON IT

BEFORE THERE WAS DAY AND NIGHT, there was only constant twilight. This did not go over well with the Day and Night Animals.

"If we're Day Animals, then where's our day?" said the Day Animals.

"And if we're Night Animals, then where's our night?" asked the Night Animals.

An argument erupted about how to divide day and night. Naturally, the Day Animals wanted all daylight, while the Night Animals wanted perpetual darkness.

What to do?

The Day and Night Animals did agree on one thing: gambling. All the Animals loved to bet, wager, lay odds, speculate, stake, and roll the dice. Give them half a chance and they would tempt fate, take a shot in the dark, count on the luck of the draw.

So to determine once and for all how to divide day and night, the Animals agreed to play their all-time favorite game of chance: the Moccasin Game. The Moccasin Game is all about guessing under which moccasin a small round stone is hidden.

Sounds easy? But no, there are rules, short cuts, 102 yucca leaves, and blankets to hide the one hiding the stone under the moccasin.

There are cedar sticks for tapping the moccasin the player thinks the stone is under, piles of sand to hide the moccasins in, and all sorts of special considerations. The Animals were completely obsessed with the Moccasin Game, and if there had been day and night, they would have played it day and night.

Each group would need a leader, so the Day Animals gambled on Coyote. Coyote was half Night Animal, but the Day Animals knew Coyote was clever and loved to win, and in a gambler, isn't that an essential quality? You bet. They knew Coyote would do whatever it took to win the game.

The Night Animals elected Owl because he was a passionate advocate for night. Owl's swift, silent wings and keen eyesight are perfect for nighttime. The Night Animals knew Owl would be their champion.

After much spirited negotiation, Owl and Coyote set the terms for the bet: If the Day Animals won, then there would be only Day. If the Night Animals won, then there would be only Night. (Coyote knew whatever happened, Day or Night, he couldn't lose!)

Coyote and Owl assembled the moccasins and all the necessary game pieces and blankets and yucca strips and various accoutrements, and found the perfect small round stone to hide. Once they were ready, they gathered all the Animals under the old cottonwood tree. The game was on!

The first guess to find the small round stone went to Badger, and she won!

Next, Squirrel guessed—right!

Possum was up next—right again.

Oriole—ding ding ding—correct!

All tied.

Raccoon—he got it right too.

Bobcat—yes!

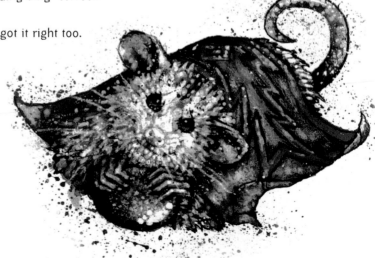

Night Day, Night Day, Night Day. Back and forth, the Night and Day Animals took turns trying to find the small round stone: Skunk, Prairie Dog; Porcupine, Rabbit; Fox, Bluebird; Wolf, Bear. For four days, the Animals played back and forth, and around they went in a dead-even heat.

But then the Night Animals went on a winning streak. Every single one of their guesses was right, yet not one of the Day Animals could guess which moccasin the small round stone was under.

Coyote, who knew a thing or two about tricks, grew suspicious.

"Time out!" he commanded. "Something shady is going on here. Where is that stone?"

No one could find the small round stone under *any* of the moccasins.

"Where is it?" cried Bluebird. The Night Animals were winning and she could not bear the thought of perpetual night.

Everyone looked under every blanket, yucca strip, pile of sand, blanket, moccasin, and rock for the small round stone. Confusion reigned. Accusations were made. Tempers flared. Just as Gopher and

Locust were about to come to fisticuffs, Coyote noticed that Owl had a funny look on his face.

Coyote sauntered over to Owl and casually noted, "Anything you want to tell us, Owl?"

Owl sheepishly ruffled his feathers and the small round stone fell to the ground. *Plop.*

Everyone gasped!

Well, could anyone really blame Owl? This was his one and only chance to win the biggest jackpot of all: endless night and a perpetual buffet.

"Nice try, Owl," said Coyote, "but it's a tie. We'll divide Day and Night equally."

And so it is.

And that's why the *Diné* tell this story only on cold winter nights, when they will hear Owl mournfully hooting over the loss of his one chance to have an endless banquet of eternal night.

And of course they will also hear Coyote, who loves both Day and Night, yipping and laughing as he bounds about under the velvety dark sky.

¤ ¤ ¤

ADAPTED FROM

Hausman, Gerald. *The Gift of the Gila Monster: Navajo Ceremonial Tales.* New York: Touchstone, 1993.
Utter, Jack. *Not an Owl, Crow, or Coyote Be: The Navajo Creation Narrative for Day and Night.* Public Books. 3 March 2015. http://www.publicbooks.org/blog/not-an-owl-crow-or-coyote-be.

Horse

COLORS OF THE SKY: THE HORSES OF THE SUN GOD

SUN GOD WAS TIRED OF WALKING the entire stretch of the sky from his hogan in the east to his hogan in the west to carry his golden disc of the sun. He convened a Council of the Holy People and said, "Surely we can come up with a better way for me to bring sunlight to the People than having me *walk* across the sky every day?"

The Holy Ones did have a better way. They created Horse. In fact, they made five horses for Sun God to ride across the sky to deliver the sun to the People. They fashioned White Shell Horse and Pearl Horse for dawn and early morning. They made Red Shell Horse for sunset and Jet Horse for night. And for the brilliant blue sky of day, they made the biggest and most glorious horse of all—Turquoise Horse.

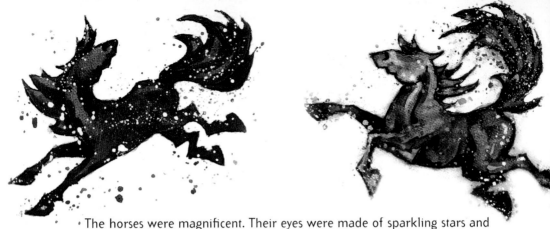

The horses were magnificent. Their eyes were made of sparkling stars and their ears of forked lightning, while their manes and tails were fashioned of soft gentle rain. Their neighs were the echo of a black flute, the brilliant sunrays their bridles, and their halters were made of rainbows. They stood upon colorful, richly woven blankets set amidst glittering grains of golden, glimmering gemstones.

But there was one problem. The horses could not move. If they could not move, then how was the Sun God to ride them across the sky to bring the sun to the People below?

"How are we going to *fix* this problem?" the Holy Gods asked each other during yet another Council meeting.

While they were deliberating, Caterpillar crawled by and overheard their dilemma.

"Excuse me Holy Ones," called Caterpillar. "Perhaps I can help. I know where to find sacred flint for the hooves."

The Holy Ones looked up. They looked to the east. The west. The north. The south. They saw no one. Who was offering help?

"I'm down here," Caterpillar called.

"Oh, there you are," the Holy Ones said, looking down at Caterpillar. "Well, can you get the flint for us?" they asked.

"I'd be delighted," Caterpillar replied, and started slowly inching his way to the Mountain of Sacred Flint.

The Holy Ones watched as Caterpillar made his way slowly, oh so very slowly, to the Mountain.

"This will take *forever*," sighed the Holy Ones.

"Caterpillar is being so obliging. Why don't we help him along a bit?" suggested Sun God. So the Holy Ones prayed over him and turned Caterpillar into a butterfly.

Caterpillar was thrilled with his newfound state of being, and swiftly flew to the Mountain of Flint. He found five sets of four flints each, and flew them back to the Holy Ones.

As Sun God carefully placed the flint in each of the horses' hooves, the horses began to prance and dance and neigh and gallop and roll about in the glimmering

grains of glittering gemstones, leaving the People below awestruck and amazed to see a golden mist drifting gently down from the sky.

Now, every day, Sun God mounts White Shell Horse in the dawn and Pearl Horse in the early morning. Ascending ever higher, just before he reaches the zenith of the sky, he mounts Turquoise Horse and rides all day until it is time for him to descend on Red Shell Horse into the sunset. Sun God then carefully covers the disc of the sun so no light escapes, while he and Jet Horse of night ride back to his hogan in the east. When they get home, he hangs the disc of the sun up on a golden peg where it waits for its return to the west the next day.

When the horses are not galloping with Sun God across the sky, they play in pastures of tall grasses and graze on the nectar of flower blossoms and drink of the fresh flowing waters of spring, rain, snow, and hail, and of the four sacred directions.

Every day, the People see the horses of the Sun God riding across the sky and are grateful for the sunlight they bring and the golden mist on the horizon that comes from the galloping of their hooves through glimmering gemstones. With gratitude, the People offer pollen and prayers to the Holy Ones and their magnificent horses.

The Holy Ones, quite pleased with the People's prayers, decided to give them the gift of the horse. Now, just like Sun God, the People no longer have to walk; they too can ride far and fast across the land.

And to this day, in thanks for the helpful role he played in bringing the sacred flint to Sun God, the hoofprints of all horses are in the shape of Caterpillar's winged self—a butterfly.

¤ ¤ ¤

ADAPTED FROM

Curtis, Natalie, ed. *The Indian's Book: Songs and Legends of the American Indian.*
    New York: Dover, 1968.

Edmonds, Margot, and Ella. E. Clark, eds. "Songs of the Horses." In *Voices of the Winds,*
    96–98. New York: Castle Books, 2003.

Haile, Father Berard. *An Ethnologic Dictionary of the Navajo Language.* St. Michaels, AZ:
    Franciscan Fathers, 1910.

Hausman, Gerald. *The Gift of the Gila Monster: Navajo Ceremonial Tales.*
    New York: Simon and Schuster, 1993.

Mose, Don, Jr. "The Legend of the Horse." *Navajo People, Culture and History.* San Juan School
    District. Accessed September 2, 2015. http://navajopeople.org/blog/the-legend-of-the-horse-book/.

Coyote

A DAZZLING DISPLAY OF COSMIC DISARRAY

IT WAS DARK. REALLY DARK. So dark that Coyote could not see his paw in front of his long nose.

"What's a night guy to do at night when he can't see a thing?" Coyote grumbled. "This has got to change."

Coyote ambled over to First Man to lobby him to add some light. First Man and First Woman were taking a much-deserved break. They had just created the Fifth World of the *Diné* and the seven sacred mountains. They were especially proud of their favorite four mountains and the special birds they had arranged to live there.

"Look at Sierra Blanca in the east," said First Man, "and all of those pigeons!"

"And Mount Taylor in the south," said First Woman. "The bluebirds are a lovely touch, dear."

"The Place of Big Mountain Sheep and the blackbirds," boasted First Man, "now there is a mountain."

"I do believe the San Francisco Peaks might be my favorite: the yellow warblers are quite exquisite," said First Woman.

Coyote was bored listening to their list of accomplishments.

"Look, First Man," Coyote interrupted, "I need some light."

"But I already let you work on the moon," said First Man, "and your foolish scheme of 'months and moon phases,' all so you and your nighttime pals can get up to your mischief."

"Yes, well, but there are nights I still can't see. Look at what a terrific job you and your lovely wife have done here with the mountains and birds. And that sun! Brilliant. What a shame it would be if we could not marvel at everything you have done both day *and* night. Don't you agree?" Coyote asked.

"He does have a good point, dear," said First Woman.

"Yes, yes, yes, fine Coyote. I'll consider your suggestion and get back to you," First Man grumbled.

Coyote thanked First Man for his consideration and slyly ambled off.

The next day, the more First Man thought about the opportunity to light up his spectacular creations, the more he liked it. Why not show off all those mountains in a different light? A diffused light. A lovely subtle light. As he was pondering how to go about this new project, the brilliant sun sparkled off the rock-star mica First Woman was using to decorate their hogan.

"That'll work," First Man thought.

He gathered up all the rock-star mica he could find and placed them in a big pile. And he made a plan. First Man always had a plan. He surveyed, plumb-lined, measured twice, and cut once. He paced out a country mile. He gauged the span of his hand, and while he was at it, he created the inch, foot, cubit, yard, acre, and a hair's breadth. He appraised a stone's throw and a hop, skip, and a jump. He calculated spitting distance. He computed, quantified, evaluated, rated, and assessed. He even asked First Woman for advice.

When he was absolutely certain his plan was perfect, he set about placing the rock-star mica carefully, oh so carefully, in the night sky. He consulted his plan and placed the very first star in the north. He wanted a star that would never move so anyone traveling at night could chart his or her course. "Even that troublemaker, Coyote," he muttered.

Then, he placed seven of the rock-star mica close to the North Star in a lovely pattern of a bear. Next he placed the bright rock stars in the south, the east, and the west. One star here, the next there, just so.

Meanwhile, Coyote, overly pleased with himself that his proposal to First Man had worked, was ready for this plan to be in place so he could get to playing at night.

"Could he take any longer?" Coyote grumbled.

"Really, First Man, we're burning daylight here," Coyote complained. "Can we move it along?"

"All must be orderly, Coyote," said First Man as he carefully placed stars in the pattern of an arrow. "That's your problem. You are always so impatient, you make a mess of everything. Why the last time . . ."

Coyote had heard enough. "Just do it this way!" Coyote shouted, and grabbed a pile of the shining mica and threw the sparkling rocks upward to the heavens.

"Coyote, stop!" First Man shouted. "These are organized patterns! I have a plan! I have calculated, computed, and quantified! I even asked First Woman! You are ruining everything!"

But impulsive, impatient Coyote was having too much fun. He grabbed pawfuls of the shining star rock and heaved them skyward, yipping and laughing with glee.

"Now there's a plan, First Man!" he shouted as the stars bounced about the heavens, falling and landing wherever they wished. By the time he had thrown all the mica into the sky, only a few of First Man's properly planned constellations remained in place.

"Oh dear," First Woman sighed as she looked up at the dazzling display of cosmic disarray. "It appears Coyote will always show us what *not* to do, by doing it."

First Man grumbled, "So much for my plans."

Meanwhile, clever, compulsive, impatient, curious, and wise Coyote was already off on his next adventure. At least he could see where he was going now.

And that is the reason all the stars are not in identifiable patterns today.

Or so it is said.

¤ ¤ ¤

ADAPTED FROM

Zolbrod, Paul. *Diné Bahane': The Navajo Creation Story.* Albuquerque: University of New Mexico Press, 1984.

Hawk, Crow, and Duck

BORED BIRDS CREATE VACATION PARADISE

IMAGINE CALIFORNIA IN THE FAR DISTANT PAST. A world completely covered with water. One tall pole standing in the water. One Hawk. One Crow. Only one perch on top of the pole in the water.

There was no love lost between Hawk and Crow, but since they were the only birds in the whole watery world, they reluctantly took turns perching on top of the pole.

"My turn!" Crow shouted.

"Not yet!" Hawk yelled.

Crow swooped low and knocked Hawk off the perch.

Hawk, fuming, flew around a bit, caught a fish for his supper from the endless waters surrounding them, and then swooped down on Crow screeching, "*My* turn!"

"Not *yet!*" Crow cawed back.

Hawk knocked Crow off the perch; Crow flew and fished for his supper and knocked Hawk off the perch.

And so it went all day—every day—for many eons of time.

One day, Crow, utterly bored with the same routine and equally bored with Hawk's company, said, "Hey, let's create more birds."

Hawk replied, "Great idea. I've had about enough of looking at you all these ages."

So Hawk and Crow created all the birds that eat fish (because in that time long ago fish were the only thing there was to eat in the whole watery world). They created Eagle and Pelican and Kingfisher and Osprey and Seagull and Heron. They also created Duck.

Duck was not interested in getting involved with the conflict over the only perch on the tall pole, but she did want to have a little place to sit that was all her own. Plus, she had an adventuresome spirit, so one day she decided to dive as deep as she could to see if there was any mud underneath all that water. She took a huge breath and dove deeper and deeper. The water got colder and colder and the light dimmer and dimmer and still she kept diving, and just when she thought she could not hold her breath a second longer, she hit bottom.

It was so dark she could not see. She quickly scooped up some of the mud with her beak and then swam and

paddled as quickly as she could
back to the surface. But it was too
late. Breathless, exhausted, and utterly
spent, she gasped out her very last words,
"There. Is. Mud. Below."

And then she died.

Stunned and saddened, for everyone had loved
Duck, the birds hovered over her lifeless body.

"She was really brave," Hawk said.

"No kidding. Now that's courage," Crow replied, and he
meant it too.

"Look, she brought the mud back in her beak,"
Hawk noted.

Hawk and Crow looked at each other, and both
realized the same thing at the same time,

"We can finally get off this pole."

Hawk and Crow gently and reverently took the mud from Duck's beak and
began making mountains. They started at the place we call today Tehachapi
Pass. They pushed and piled and packed the mud into the form of mountains.
And because they loved Duck and honored her sacrifice, there was a never-
ending supply of mud.

Hawk piled the mud to make the mountains to the east by the rising sun,
while Crow piled the mud to the west by the setting sun. Moving north, they

pushed and piled and packed the mud for many ages of time, until finally, one sunny clear afternoon, they met at the mountain that today we call Mount Shasta.

Exhausted but proud of their efforts, they rested and made a toast to Duck: "All ducks will forevermore have her adventuresome spirit!"

But then Hawk's keen eyes settled on Crow's mountains to the west, and he frowned.

"Why is your mountain range so much bigger than mine?" Hawk demanded.

Crow smirked.

"You cheating scoundrel!" Hawk cried. "You have been stealing mud from *my* mountains when I was not looking. That's why your mountains are bigger than mine!"

Crow laughed.

"I'll show *you*," Hawk said. He took hold of the mountains in his strong beak and turned them around in a circle. He put his mountain range where Crow's had been, and Crow's where his had been. So now, the mountains in the east were much higher than the mountains in the west.

"So there," Hawk said and he spread his wings and flew high into the sky to perch on the top of the highest peak in his mountain range next to the rising sun.

And that is why today, thanks to a brave, adventuresome duck and two bored birds, in the mountains of California, the Sierra Nevada range to the east is much higher than the Coastal Range to the west.

¤ ¤ ¤
ADAPTED FROM

Judson, Katherine. "Origin of the Sierra Nevadas and Coast Range." In *Myths and Legends of California*, 9. Chicago: McClurg, 1913.

Bat

ONLY THOSE WHO OBEY CAN COMMAND

THE DEAL WITH MONSTER SLAYER was that he would make
Bat Woman beautiful if she would get him down off the very high cliff ledge.
One half of the famous Hero Twins, Monster Slayer was named for—wait for
it—slaying monsters. His twin brother is named He Who Cuts the Life Out of
the Enemy. That's a different story, but suffice it to say their legendary mom,
Changing Woman, is quite proud.

Monster Slayer was on the high cliff ledge because he had just killed Bird
Monster—a clever and brave thing to do—but he had not quite thought it all
the way through. So there he was, stuck on the ledge, with the only way down
requiring wings of some sort. He had quite a few feathers, all of Bird Monster's
in fact, but they were still stuck to the deceased body of Bird Monster.

He noticed a small figure walking along the cliff ledge below him. It was
Bat Woman.

"Grandmother Bat Woman!" he called. "Up here, see me? I am stuck! Can you please help me?"

Bat Woman peered up, saw Monster Slayer looking at her, and shouted, "Don't look at me! I am ugly!" and darted behind the ledge.

"Odd," thought Monster Slayer.

But Bat Woman's fear of people thinking her ugly was trumped by her curiosity, so she peeked up from behind the ledge again.

"I see you Grandmother," Monster Slayer called. "Please, it's getting dark and I am stuck up here!"

Bat Woman peeked out and disappeared again and again. Then she hid behind a rock, and shouted again, "Don't look at me! I am ugly!"

Monster Slayer realized this game might go on for some time. He was a quick study though, so he used the one thing he had to negotiate with. "Bat Woman, if you help me, I will give you the feathers of Bird Monster."

Bat Woman poked her head out. "Why would I want those?" she asked suspiciously, and darted back behind the rock.

"Because they will make you beautiful," Monster Slayer gently replied.

Well, what woman is going to say no to that offer? Especially Bat Woman, with her leathery skin and webbed feet and arms. It did not matter what she did for anyone (and she did quite a lot), the first thing anyone ever said about her was, "Yes she is helpful, but she is so ugly."

Here was a chance to change that. Forever.

"Close your eyes. Don't look at me. I am too ugly. But, I will help you if you listen and do exactly as I say," she commanded Monster Slayer. "Get in my basket and I will fly you to the bottom of the cliff. But you must keep your eyes closed."

"Are you serious?" Monster Slayer exclaimed. "With all due respect, that basket is huge, I'm a big guy, and you are very small."

"Do as I say! Do you not trust me? Am I too ugly and small to help you?"

"No, no," stammered Monster Slayer. He had just slain one of the biggest monsters in the *Diné* world, but clearly he had met his match in Bat Woman.

Well, after testing the weight of the basket with stones, and arguing back and forth about the wisdom of a very heavy guy being flown off a cliff by a very small bat, and some more haranguing by Bat Woman, Monster Slayer finally got into the basket.

"Keep your eyes shut. Do not look," she said.

He shut his eyes tight, gripped the sides of the basket, and Bat Woman flew into the twilight sky, dangling the basket with Monster Slayer and the recently departed Bird Monster stuffed inside. But her wings made the strangest sound, so of course he had to open his eyes to look. The minute he did, the basket started to fall.

"Close them! I told you to keep them shut!" she shouted.

"OK! OK!" Monster Slayer obediently shut his eyes and gripped the side of the basket even harder.

But then Bat Woman started zigging and zagging across the sky, her wings cutting a downward pattern to the bottom, and that was too intriguing not to see, so once again Monster Slayer opened his eyes.

"If you do not listen to me, I will drop this basket!" she threatened.

Monster Slayer knew she meant it. He sighed, crossed his fingers for luck, and kept his eyes shut tight as Bat Woman flapped her leathery wings and zigged and zagged him safely to a perfect landing at the bottom of the cliff.

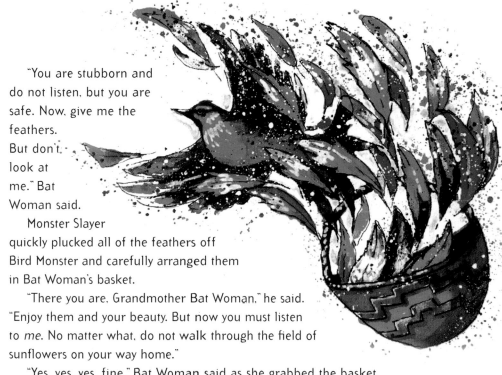

"You are stubborn and
do not listen, but you are
safe. Now, give me the
feathers.
But don't
look at
me." Bat
Woman said.

Monster Slayer
quickly plucked all of the feathers off
Bird Monster and carefully arranged them
in Bat Woman's basket.

"There you are, Grandmother Bat Woman," he said.
"Enjoy them and your beauty. But now you must listen
to *me*. No matter what, do not walk through the field of
sunflowers on your way home."

"Yes, yes, yes, fine," Bat Woman said as she grabbed the basket.
But she was so excited to become beautiful that in her hurry to get home
she walked straight through the field of sunflowers.

"Bat Woman! No! Get out of the sunflower field!" Monster Slayer shouted
after her.

But all Bat Woman could hear were her many future admirers declaring,
"Oh you are so beautiful!" She was too busy thinking about how everyone

would love her when she was pretty. As she walked
through the sunflower field dreaming of how
popular she would be, a feather fluttered out
of her basket and turned into a beautiful
golden Oriole.

And then another feather flew out
and became a vibrant Bluebird the
color of the sky.

And then another, a ruby-red
Cardinal. Another, a Rufous-sided
Towhee. Another, a Mockingbird. Then a Blue Jay. Then an
iridescent Hummingbird, and
another and another and
another. Every feather
turned into a beautiful
bird and flew into
the sunflowers. When she
realized what was happening,
Bat Woman flitted about the
sunflower field reaching
for the feathers, clutching
only empty air, until all

the feathers in Bat Woman's basket had fluttered out and become birds—all the birds the *Diné* know today.

Not one feather was left in her basket.

Bat Woman knew her chance to be beautiful was gone forever. She knelt to the ground with her empty basket and wept.

Monster Slayer, watching from afar, had tears in his eyes too. Bat Woman had helped him, and he knew she longed to be beautiful. "Ah, Grandmother Bat Woman," he said sadly, "if one will be listened to, then one must also listen."

And that is how the beautiful birds came to be, from the feathers of Bird Monster, and the beauty that might have been Bat Woman's.

And that is why, too, to this day, Bat Woman hides in cracks and crevices and only comes out at night. She cannot bear for anyone to see her and call her ugly.

¤ ¤ ¤

ADAPTED FROM

Zolbrod, Paul. *Diné Bahane': The Navajo Creation Story.* Albuquerque: University of New Mexico Press, 1984.

Butterfly

THE ART OF CREATING BUTTERFLIES

CREATOR WAS SITTING ON THE FRONT PORCH on a nice fall day, watching the village children play. He observed the little girls skipping and the young boys romping and the frisky puppies frolicking. They were happy and carefree, and Creator marveled at their youth and innocence.

But Creator could feel the bittersweet hint of autumn in the air. "It changes in just one day it seems," he thought, "that slant in the light that means that summer is over and winter is coming. How very sad that nothing stays the same. One day, those little girls will be wrinkled and gray and bent. The boys will have creaky knees and a wide seat." Creator sighed. "This aging thing is not always a treat."

Creator was growing more despondent. "Those puppies will get fleas, the flower petals will wilt, and the leaves will fall and die. What have I done?" he moaned. "If all beauty fades and everything changes, then what is the point?"

But he was the Creator, after all, so he had some clout. "Lighten up, buddy" Creator said to himself, "and create."

He marveled at the intense shade of blue sky that heralds fall. The sun felt warm on his face. The leaves might be falling, but they were sure pretty as they glowed with a golden sheen in the autumnal sunshine. Creator had an idea. He grabbed a big tote bag to fill and started selecting items from everything he had created.

"Sunbeams? Yes!"

"That perfect shade of autumn sky?" he mused. "Hmm, cerulean? Turquoise? Teal? Cobalt? Royal? Cornflower? Ultramarine? Indigo? Sapphire?"

"Yep, sapphire. That's it," and he added sapphire blue to his tote bag.

"Next? White cornmeal."

He asked the group of women kneading cornmeal for corncakes.

"Ladies, may I borrow a pinch?"

They giggled as he flirted with them, and he noticed the blue/black sheen from their shiny hair and added a lock to the bag with the cornmeal.

Then, he shaved off some of the golden yellow gleam from the fallen leaves.

Next, he plucked a plethora of petals from the fanciful fall flowers—scarlet, ruby, crimson, burnt orange, all shades of purple—lavender, violet, periwinkle. And while he was at it, he added some yellow pollen from the sunflowers.

Finally, he sprinkled deep-green pine needles on top of the bag, and shook it well.

"Oops, forgot sound!" he said, reopened the tote and added the songs of all the birds, then shook again.

Creator was quite pleased with his handiwork. He had forgotten all about winter coming. "Children!" he called. "Quick, come see what I have made for you!"

The children gathered around in excitement. When they opened the bag, out flew the very first butterflies, with wings the colors of the flower petals and pine needles and white cornmeal and shiny black hair and golden rays of sun. Everyone laughed and danced with joy.

And then the butterflies started to sing! The children danced and giggled and clapped their hands with delight.

But pretty and delightful as the butterflies were, Creator had added something he should not have: the songs of all the birds. Soon, a flock of angry birds had gathered, chirping and tweeting and twittering.

"You promised each bird we would have our own song," said Oriole, "and now you have given my song to this, this, *scaly-winged* thing."

"Isn't it enough that they already have shiny golden wings?" said plain, gray Sparrow.

"Really, Creator?" Blue Jay squawked. "You'll be hearing from my guy on the tribal council."

"Yeah," said Mockingbird, "you'll be hearing from my guy on the tribal council."

At that, all the birds started arguing among themselves, and a cacophony of angry squawks, tweets, chirps, cheeps, screeches, and peeps (but no songs) engulfed Creator, the children, the puppies, and the butterflies.

Creator realized he had blown it.

"Enough!" he shouted. He snapped his fingers and the songs left the butterflies and flew back to their original owners.

Satisfied, the songbirds adjusted their ruffled feathers and flew off happily singing their songs. Creator watched the happy children dancing

with joy, and the fragile butterflies flying in the autumn sunlight, and in that one perfect moment, he thought to himself, "All is well."

And that is how and why the beautiful, but silent, butterflies came to be.

¤ ¤ ¤

ADAPTED FROM

Bruchac, Joseph. "How the Butterflies Came to Be." In *Native American Indian Stories*, 45–47. Golden, CO: Fulcrum, 1992.

Erdoes, Richard, and Alfonso Ortiz, eds. "Butterflies." In *American Indian Myths and Legends*, 407–408. New York: Pantheon, 1984.

Deer

DRESSED FOR SUCCESS: SURVIVAL TOOLS
OF THE ANIMAL PEOPLE

WAKAN TANKA, GREAT CREATOR OF THE LAKOTA SIOUX, cared deeply for all of the Animal People. But as any Creator does, he worried and fussed and had some sleepless nights over their well-being.

"What if an enemy attacks them?" he thought anxiously. "They need to have survival tools to protect themselves. I should ask each animal what they prefer and give them what they need."

So he surveyed, polled, interviewed, questioned, interrogated, and quizzed each of the animals to see what survival equipment would best suit them.

"I can pounce and I have big paws," said Mountain Lion. "How about some really sharp claws?"

"I am a big guy," said Grizzly Bear. "Why not give me brawn and muscle to fight my enemy?"

"Sharper teeth," said Wolf, as he grinned, showing off his canines.

"I'm not brawny, nor do I have sharp teeth, and I am not much for fighting," said Coyote slyly. "I'd like cleverness."

"Done, done, done, and done," said Wakan Tanka. (Although he and all of the Animal and Lakota People would later wish he had not given Coyote all that cleverness.)

"How about you, Beaver?" asked Wakan Tanka.

"My flat tail is good for whacking someone, but I could use some webbed feet for diving beneath the water," Beaver said.

"Done," agreed Wakan Tanka.

Porcupine chimed in, "I'm a bit on the slow side. How about if my quills can be really sharp and stick in my enemy and be really hard to pull out?"

"Great idea!" said Wakan Tanka. "Done."

"Rabbit?" Wakan Tanka asked.

"*Everybody* seems to be my enemy, so I need to run as swiftly as possible," Rabbit said nervously. "Can you put some spring in my hind legs so I can get up and go quickly?"

"Done!" said Wakan Tanka. "This is fun!" he thought.

"Birds? Clearly, wings are for flying, floating, diving, and escaping. Plus you have talons and sharp beaks. Is that OK with everyone?" Wakan Tanka asked.

"Perfect!" all the birds tweeted, chirped, peeped, hooted, and cawed.

Mother Deer shyly approached the Creator with her newborn fawn close to her side. "You have given me long legs with the ability to leap over obstacles, jump high, and run swiftly, so that is all ideal for me," she said.

"Great!" Wakan Tanka said, pleased that it had worked out so well for Deer.

"But Wakan Tanka, my baby fawn here is utterly helpless against the

teeth and claws and strength and cleverness of her many enemies. What can you do for her?"

Wakan Tanka surveyed the wobbly newborn fawn carefully. "Hmmm, she's a tricky one. But I have an idea." And he mixed up some paint from the rocks and the plants and the sky and the trees and the flowers and the earth and the tall prairie grass and made some swatches and held them up to Fawn's coat.

"Too dark, too light, too much yellow, too much brown, needs more green— wait, this is just right!" and he took the just-right shade of the surrounding rocks and plants and sky and trees and flowers and earth and tall prairie grass, and painted the newborn fawn's coat with spots.

Now she blended in perfectly with everything around her.

"When your mom is not with you," Wakan Tanka said to Fawn, "you must stay absolutely still and then no one will be able to see you."

Fawn solemnly blinked her big brown eyes and shyly whispered, "Yes, sir."

"Oh, and wait!" Wakan Tanka leaned over Fawn and drew a long, deep breath, completely removing her scent. "There, now no one will get a whiff of you either," he said, quite satisfied with his work.

Now Fawn is safe if she stays completely still when her mom is away. And when she grows up, her perfectly blended spots will fade, and she will have the other survival tools of the Deer People, the gift of swiftness and speed to outrun her enemy.

And now that Wakan Tanka has given all of his Animal People the right survival equipment, he can finally get a good night's sleep.

¤ ¤ ¤

ADAPTED FROM

Bruchac, Joseph. "How the Fawn Got Its Spots." In *Native American Indian Stories*, 89–90. Golden, CO: Fulcrum, 1992.

Dolphin

SOMEWHERE UNDER THE RAINBOW

––––––––––––

HUTASH SOWED THE SEEDS FROM HER MAGIC PLANT, creating the very first Chumash People on Santa Cruz Island. It was just the sort of art project an Earth Goddess loved to do.

But it was not long before the People were cold and grew tired of eating only raw foods.

"Dear?" Hutash asked her husband, Sky Snake. "Would you mind giving fire to my sweet Chumash People?"

Sky Snake—we know him today as the Milky Way—was always looking for the perfect gift for his wife. "I'd love to, honey," he said, and sent a lightning bolt full of star-fire to the Island, igniting the very first fire for the People.

Fire is an element that changes everything. Fire means no more cold, chilly nights spent huddling together to stay warm. Fire means an expanded dinner menu. Fire means the heat to make pots of clay. Fire extended the day into

night and kept those pesky mosquitos away. Fire meant beacons lit on mountaintops to relay messages and light to gather around for stories. Fire kept scary things away. Fire meant hot tea and boiled fiesta eggs and roasted acorns and popped corn. Fire meant making silly shadow figures and sealing wax and torches for midnight rendezvous. Sky Snake's gift of star-fire was better than any other present he could have found in the entire galaxy.

Hutash was delighted her People could be warm, fed, protected, and comfortable. The People and Animal People were delighted too. Except for poor Condor! He was so curious about fire that he swooped down low to take a closer look, and all of his pure white feathers turned a sooty black. To this day, Condor has only a little white left on his wings where the fire did not scorch him. He's still embarrassed about it too, which is why he is seldom seen and stays away from people.

Except for Condor's embarrassment, all was well. The People were comfy and cozy, and when people are comfy and cozy, that means more babies are born. So over time, the villages on the island got bigger, more crowded, and noisy.

Hutash was not happy about this.

"I love my children," she complained to Sky Snake, "but all the noise is giving me a headache and they are keeping me up all night."

"Why don't you send some of them off the island to the mainland?" Sky Snake suggested.

"Oh honey," Hutash brightened up considerably, "what a lovely idea."

But, how was she to move them? The People had small fishing boats that only held one or two, certainly not big enough for all the aunties and uncles and cousins and grandfolks. It was too far to swim, and this was long before people could sky travel.

Then Hutash had another idea. "What if I create a bridge made of a rainbow?" she asked Sky Snake. "I can start it at the highest peak on the island and have it stretch all the way to the highest mountaintop on the mainland coast."

"Splendid, darling," Sky Snake replied.

So Hutash created a shimmering rainbow high across the sky, spanning the ocean waters of the Pacific from Santa Cruz Island to the highest mountain peak on the mainland shore by Carpinteria.

She told the People all about their new home on the mainland and invited them to move. It was a big decision for families to move away from aunties and uncles and cousins and grandfolks. Some decided to make the trip, while others chose to stay on the island. Those who were leaving lined up with their most treasured belongings to walk across the Rainbow Bridge, tears in their eyes as they said goodbye to family.

Hutash packed them snacks and wished them bon voyage, and as they were leaving called after them. "Do not look down, my dears! It is quite far and you might fall. Be careful!"

Most made it across safely.

But imagine being high in the sky on a rainbow bridge of shimmering color and light, with Santa Cruz Island and everyone you know to your back and the mainland stretching before you in front. Wouldn't it be hard not to look down? Of course it would, and some people did. And they got dizzy and disoriented and fell far below into the cold waters of the Pacific Ocean.

When Hutash saw her People falling off the bridge into the cold deep sea, she was horrified. "Oh no!" she cried. "You must not drown and die!" And to save her beloved People from drowning, she conjured up perhaps her most important creation: she turned them into dolphins.

That is why, to this day, there are always dolphins frolicking between Santa Cruz Island and the shore of the mainland: they are the relatives of the Chumash People, traveling back and forth in the sparkling waters of the Pacific to visit their kin.

¤ ¤ ¤

ADAPTED FROM

Redish, Laura, and Orrin Lewis, eds. "The Rainbow Bridge: A Chumash Legend." *Native Languages of the Americas: Chumash Legends, Myths and Stories*, edited by Camp Internet's Nipumu Village Project. Accessed July 3, 2015. www.native-languages.org; www.rain.org/camp96/chumash1.html.

Raven

ETERNAL SUMMER? NEVERMORE.

THE PRIEST YANAULUHA CARRIED A MAJESTIC STAFF decorated with feathers and plumes of deep blue and green, bright yellow, iridescent black, and vibrant red. Seashells and treasures and trinkets dangled from the staff and tinkled and chimed whenever Yanauluha moved.

The People were entranced by this charmed staff and gathered around, stretching their hands to touch and stroke the feathers and trinkets, and perhaps capture some of the magic.

Yanauluha would not let the People touch the sacred staff, but he did have a gift for them. He blew on the staff so the feathers fluttered and all the trinkets chimed as one; then he struck the staff to the ground hard and suddenly there appeared four eggs. Two were sky blue and sparkled and glittered like sunlight on the sea. Two were dull brownish-red: the color of the land surrounding the People.

"What are they?" the People asked in awe.

"In these eggs dwell the leaders you will follow. From two eggs will emerge great beings of Summer with the most beautiful colorful plumage. If you choose those eggs, then you will follow their flight to a faraway land of eternal summer. You will never toil in the fields for food, for all crops will flourish without any work on your part."

"Endless vacation!" said the People in a collective sigh of delight.

"In the other two eggs dwell the beings of Winter, tricksters of pure black. Where they fly you will follow and winter will always be in rival with summer. The fields will flourish only with your hard labor and that of your children and your children's children forevermore.

"Choose wisely," Yanauluha cautioned.

"Well, that's easy," some of the People said. Naturally, they believed the Summer beings would be in the eggs the color of the sparkling, glittering sea. So the strongest of the people pushed their way to Yanauluha and demanded the dazzling sky-blue eggs. They gently took the precious eggs and lay them in a nest of soft sand in

the full bright sun and took turns waiting expectantly for the beautiful birds to hatch.

Those who had waited a bit and not pushed to the front were left with the dull brownish-red eggs.

When the glittering sky-blue eggs cracked open, the birds emerged, and their skin, for they had no feathers just yet, glistened with colors of sea green and blue, sunny yellow, red, and lush tropical green. The People were ecstatic. "We chose wisely!" they proclaimed to the brownish-red group. "No more work for us! No more Winter! Vacation always!" they said with glee. And they fed the growing birds with all of the foods they themselves liked to eat, so the birds knew to eat what the People ate.

But as the precious birds matured, something strange happened. Their feathers grew in and all the colors faded into one: black. Then the People knew their birds were Ravens: the birds of Winter.

The Ravens laughed and cawed and croaked and mocked the People for their self-indulgence and greed. The Ravens collected glittery trinkets and treasures and ate everything the People ate, for, after all, isn't that what was expected of them from the very start?

Meanwhile, the birds of the brownish-red eggs emerged as beautiful, colorful Macaws, and the priest Yanauluha, with a flick of his sacred staff, wafted the beautiful Macaws and the People who had chosen so wisely and carefully to the far distant and eternal lands of Summer, the lands of endless vacation and no toil. The Summer People were fewer in number, and not as hardy as the Winter People, but because they were deliberate and patient, their wisdom was rewarded.

And those who chose Raven became the Raven People. They were the people of Winter and toil, and they were many. But because they were strong and opinionated, the Ravens—although they loved to mock and tease and trick them—loved the Winter People too. After all, the Ravens were a reflection of the People's hopes and dreams. And what is black but all the colors mixed together? And what are trinkets and treasures but something special to someone? And what is glitter but the reflection of sunlight on the ordinary and mundane?

The Ravens knew all this and taught the People, and for their magic and own special wisdom, the People grew to love them.

As for loving Winter and all that toil? Not so much.

¤ ¤ ¤

ADAPTED FROM

Judson, Katherine, ed. "Origin of Raven and Macaw." In *Myths and Legends of California*, 154. Chicago: McClurg, 1913.

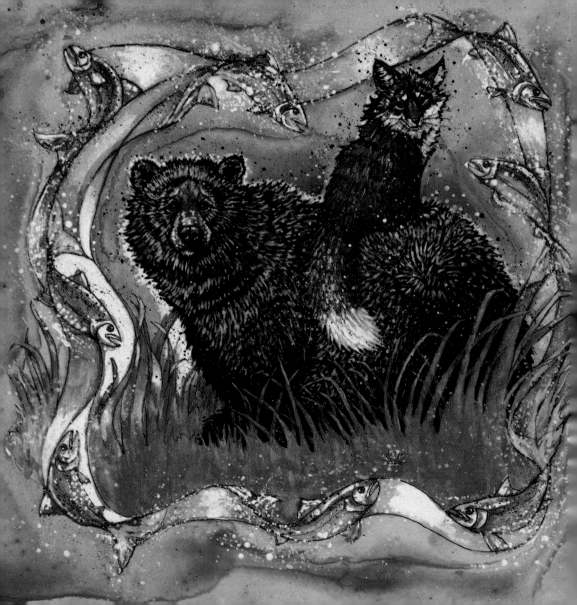

Bear and Fox

A FISHY STORY:
HOW BEAR LOST HIS BEAUTIFUL LONG TAIL

BEAR WAS HUNGRY.

"Fish sounds good," he thought. So he made his way over to the river. It was chilly out, and ice lined the river, especially in the shady spots. But the sun was bright and Bear could see the fish under the sparkling water.

"Yum!" he thought and sat down to catch his lunch. He used his rod and reel. No luck.

"Hmmm," he thought. "I'll just use my big bear paws." Still no luck. So he fly-fished. No bites. "What is going on here?!" Bear said, irritated. He netted, angled, trapped, and whittled a spear out of an aspen branch. Still nothing. He jigged, trolled, bottom-bounced, chummed, and dredged. He trout-tickled. He even asked Eagle to fly over the river for some aerial surveillance. Not one bite.

Dejected and hungry, he saw Fox, who happened to be carrying a line of ten fish he had just caught.

"Fox!" Bear called. "How did you catch all of those fish?"

Now, Fox is cousin to Coyote, and playing a good joke on someone is part of the family legacy. Plus, in the universal language of jokesters, Fox recognized a perfect opportunity when he saw one.

"Aren't you supposed to be a great fisherman?" Fox asked.

"Harumph," Bear replied proudly, "does a bear fish in the woods? Of course I am!"

"Of course," Fox said soothingly. "Perhaps the bright sun was distracting the fish. Some say it is best to fish on a cloudy day, but what do I know?"

"You know something," Bear replied, "you have ten fish."

"Bear, because you are my friend," Fox said, "I will share with you a secret you must not tell anyone else. All you have to do is sit on the ice and put your tail in the river. The fish will simply grab onto your tail, and then when you get up, they will be hanging there. With your lovely long tail just like mine, you should be able to catch dozens of fish!"

Bear was exceptionally proud of his long silky tail, and said, "You are right, Fox. My tail is even longer than yours! I bet I can get many fish to grab onto my tail. Thank you very much." And Bear lumbered back to the river to fish with his tail.

Bear did not see Fox laughing as he made his way back to the river. He found a good place on the ice next to a large boulder in the middle of the river. He carefully situated himself on the boulder and let his long glorious tail float in the water. He sat and sat and waited and waited, but there were no fish grabbing hold of his tail. So, he moved to another spot and tried again.

"My tail is really cold in this icy water," he thought, "but it will be worth it to catch all those fish!"

Well, of course he was not going to catch any fish with his tail, and when he got up, he discovered that he could not feel his tail anymore; it was completely numb. That's because his gorgeous long tail had frozen off

and was floating in the water. All he had left was a short little bobbed tail.

Bear was heartbroken. His beautiful tail was his pride and joy. "Fox! You tricked me!" he cried. He ran back to the woods to find Fox—easy to do; he had only to follow the smell of frying fish.

"Fox! My long beautiful tail has frozen off," Bear cried. "How would you feel if you lost your long beautiful tail?"

Fox was horrified to see Bear with a short little bobbed tail. He had just wanted to play a good joke on Bear so he could tell Coyote. He had not meant for Bear's tail to freeze off. Fox turned and looked at his own long glorious tail, and with a shudder, realized how upset he would be to lose it.

"Bear, I'm so sorry. I just wanted to play a little joke on you," Fox said. "Please, let me make it up to you. You can have all of my fish for your supper."

Bear was so upset about his tail that he could use a little comfort food, so he sat down and ate all of the fish and warmed his short little bobbed tail by Fox's fire.

Fox was so embarrassed and ashamed that he never told his cousin Coyote about the joke. And Bear was so embarrassed that he had fallen for the joke, that he never told anyone either.

But the fish, who were not happy to be part of the whole tail drama, told everyone they knew. So now everyone knows why, thanks to a very fishy practical joke, bears have short bobbed tails.

¤ ¤ ¤

ADAPTED FROM

Begay, Sandra. "Why the Bear Has a Short Tail." In *And It Is Still That Way*, edited by Byrd Baylor, 11. Tuba City Boarding School. New York: Charles Scribner, 1976.

"Why the Bear Has a Short Tail." *Book of Nature Myths*. Internet Sacred Text Archive. Evinity Publishing Inc. Accessed August 20, 2015. http://www.sacred-texts.com/etc/bnm/bnm22.htm.

Rattlesnake

GOOD INTENTIONS AND REPTILIAN REPUTATIONS

A YOUNG BOY WAS OUT FOR AN EARLY WALK on a cold, frosty morning when he spotted a rattlesnake stretched out stiff as a branch, encased in solid ice.

"Oh no!" cried the tenderhearted boy. "The poor rattlesnake has frozen solid."

The boy knew better than to ever, *ever* touch one of the Rattlesnake People, frozen or not, but he was curious to see if the snake was still alive, so he picked up a twig and poked the snake.

"Pleassse help me! I am sssssoo cold," Rattlesnake hissed.

The boy shrieked and leapt as far away from the snake as possible. "You're alive!" the boy said.

"Well, not for much longer if you don't help me," said the shivering snake.

"What can I possibly do? You are one of the Rattlesnake People and I am not to touch you."

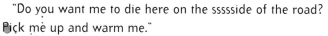

"Do you want me to die here on the ssssside of the road? Pick me up and warm me."

"But you are a *rattlesnake*!" the boy cried. "Your People bite my People!"

"Well yesss, that has on occasssssion happened. But I will not bite you," Rattlesnake said through chattering teeth. "But I will die if you do not pick me up and get me warm. Pleassse? Do you want to live with my death on your conssscience?"

"Well," said the boy. And against his better judgment and all he had learned and his instincts and intuition and his mother's admonitions about touching rattlesnakes and his father's warnings about touching rattlesnakes and any story he had ever read or been told around the storyteller's fire and the "Don't Touch the Rattlesnake People No Matter What They Tell You Because They Will Bite," signs posted everywhere he went, he picked up the rattlesnake and held him close against his woolen jacket to warm him up.

Slowly, the snake defrosted and thawed and became supple and stretchy and flexible against the warm wool of the boy's jacket.

And then, without even a warning rattle, *Boom!* Just like that, the rattlesnake bit the young boy right on the arm.

"Owwww! You bit me!" the boy yelped. "Really, Rattlesnake? I *helped* you!

I *saved* you! You said you would not bite me!" He cried in disbelief, clutching his bitten arm.

"Ah, yessss, I am very sssorry about that," Rattlesnake replied. "But, you *knew* I was a rattlesssnake when you touched me," he added matter-of-factly, as he slithered, warm and toasty, into the sagebrush and disappeared.

And so, that is why even if a Rattlesnake Person tells you he will not bite, it is his nature to do so. And that is why it is said that when someone shows you who they are, it is best to believe them.

¤ ¤ ¤

ADAPTED FROM

Bruchac, Joseph. "The Boy and the Rattlesnake." In *Native American Indian Stories*, 61–62. Golden, CO: Fulcrum, 1992.

Turkey

TURKEY SAVES THANKSGIVING
FOR EVERYONE BUT HIMSELF

AS PER USUAL, THE CHAOS WAS ALL COYOTE'S DOING.
In what he was calling an "unfortunate misunderstanding," Coyote had
accidentally kidnapped Water Monster's two babies during a high-stakes poker
game, and Water Monster, taking understandable umbrage, had retaliated by
flooding the Fourth World.

First Woman, an effective organizer, having already moved her people from
the Third World, quickly assembled all thirty-two clans, as well as all of the
Animal and Bird People. (The Water People could swim of course.) Everyone
agreed with the number one rule on First Woman's moving list: *If the Current
World Floods, Then It Is Time to Leave.* And they made plans with haste.

"And you Wise Men of the thirty-two clans," First Woman added, "find some
magic to get us out of here to the next world."

The Wise Men looked at the rapidly approaching floodwaters and then at each other and said, "We're on it."

For four days the Wise Men prayed and chanted over magic seeds that grew into a huge hollow reed that reached into the new world and could fit everyone inside.

Relieved, First Woman checked "Find Magic," off her list.

The floodwaters were hissing and boiling, and the waves were lapping and leaping into the homes of the People. Just imagine the fear and chaos as everyone ran to pack up their most precious valuables and retreat up the mountain, all to the constant refrain of Coyote saying, "It's not my fault!"

Turkey could hear the angry voice of Water Monster in the water, and knew something bad had happened. "Has to be Coyote's fault," he surmised correctly, as, not sure what to do, he watched everyone running about grabbing what they could.

"Bring whatever you want to have in the new world and go to the mountain."
Spider Woman shouted at Turkey as she
grabbed silk thread for rope and blankets.
"And hurry! The water is almost here!"

Turkey saw Bear with his paws full
of nuts, and Owl with her herbs
for medicine. Gopher had pottery
clay in four different colors, while
Packrat had stashed her favorite

cactus and yucca fruit, and even tied them up with a pretty piece of sky-blue yarn that someone had dropped. Porcupine was bringing quills and pine pitch, while Canary, Lark, and Oriole had wildflowers and pollen.

"What do I want to bring to the new world," Turkey asked himself, thinking hard. "Well of course, delicious food!"

Turkey had grown quite fat (he preferred the term *fluffy*), due to his tendency to overindulge on the snacks First Woman spoiled him with. Due to his fluffiness, he was short of breath if he attempted too much activity, and all that fluffiness meant he could not fly much either. But, he did cut a handsome figure as he strutted about the yard.

As he strutted quickly back home to pack some snacks, he noticed the storeroom door was ajar, and peeked inside to see the pottery jars full of seeds packed carefully on each of the four walls.

"Hmmm, no one has thought to bring the seeds," he noted.

And suddenly the enormity of what was happening hit him fully, and he realized this move was not about packing some corncakes to munch on the trip up the mountain. "We will need food in the new world or we will all *starve to death*," he said, horrified. "And *no one* has thought to bring the seeds!"

Turkey could hear the angry voice of Water Monster in the waves and knew he had little time. He looked at the heavy jars and realized there was no way he could carry them. "Alright then, I'll have to put the seeds under my feathers."

Turkey opened the jar on the east wall to find every kind and color of corn kernels. He was so anxious that he made himself think of something other than the floodwaters. "Corn! Let's see. I can have corn dogs, corn-flakes, corn fritters, popcorn, pudding corn, corn soup, corn bread, and creamed corn!"

When he had gathered all the corn seeds, he moved to the south wall. "Beans! Black, pinto, white, beeweed. And even sunflower seeds, yum, my favorite," he thought, and despite the approaching flood, his mouth watered.

Next he turned to the west wall: "Squash, melon, gourd, pumpkin, onion. Blech, onion. But First Woman likes it," he said to himself as he tucked the onion seed safely under his wing.

The water was getting closer, and he was running out of room to store the seeds under his feathers. "Whatever can I leave behind?" he wailed. Turkey could not bear the thought of leaving *any* of the precious seeds, so he opened the jar on the north wall that held tobacco, mustard, sage, mint, and peppergrass, and stuffed those seeds into the feathers under his chin.

By the time he had safely situated each seed, he waddled out of the storeroom to find himself utterly alone: everyone had left to climb the mountain. He could hear the angry hiss of the floodwaters rapidly approaching.

"Oh dear," he said, and headed toward the mountain, keeping his wings tight against him so no seeds were lost. Turkey was slow on a good day, and he was so weighed down with all the seeds he could barely move.

"I'll never make it," he sighed with despair. "Help! Someone please help me!"

"I'll help you, Turkey," sighed Wind, as he pushed him from behind.

"We'll help too," said the Chaparral Bushes as they bent backward so Turkey could pass.

"I'll help you too, dear," said Earth. "Let me move these big stones out of your way."

"Oh thank you, thank you!" Turkey cried, his face bright red as he gasped and wheezed his way up the mountain with Wind pushing and Bushes bending and Earth clearing and the angry floodwaters splashing and gurgling at his feet.

Meanwhile, all of the thirty-two clans and the Animal and Bird People had made it to the top inside the magic reed, and were all checked off First Woman's list. Except Turkey. Anxiously, she scanned the trail, and finally saw him struggling up the mountain path.

"Turkey!" she shouted. "Hurry! The waters are right behind you!"

Turkey, bedraggled, exhausted, splashed with mud and foam, puffed and panted his way up the mountain trail. Everyone had gathered at the door and were shouting, "Hurry, Turkey, hurry!"

He *just* made it. As he stumbled through the door of the great hollow reed, Water Monster roared and reached out to grab Turkey's tail with his foamy fingers, leaving a ragged line of white that Turkey was never able to get out.

Wind Man blew the door shut just in time, and Water Monster's angry waters roiled and boiled and splashed in vain against the door.

Turkey plopped onto the ground, so out of breath, all he could say was, "Gobble, gobble."

Now that all were safely in the hollow reed, First Woman said, "Let's see what we have for the new world."

Everyone had their favorite useful item to help create a brand new world not covered with angry water. Duck brought his favorite water tubers. Ant carried grass seeds. Bluebird, turquoise; Mountain Jay, white shell and jet; Mourning Dove, red dye and leather for moccasins.

First Man brought his medicine bundle and his freshly sharpened stone knife. First Woman packed her weaving sticks and spindle.

And, as always, Coyote brought Trouble.

"What about you Turkey?" Coyote taunted. "What do you have? I see nothing with you but your fat lazy self."

You could have heard a seed drop.

And they did. As Turkey pushed himself up, looked Coyote right in the eye, and slowly, carefully, spread his wings, all the seeds fell to the floor. The corn and beans and squash and pumpkin and mint, even the onion—all of the precious seeds that would supply the food for the Fifth World. After every last seed had been shaken out, Turkey carefully folded his wings, adjusted his feathers and said with great dignity, "I'm not fat. I'm fluffy." Then he turned and walked away.

At that moment, all of the thirty-two clans and the Animal and Bird People realized the same thing at the same time: if Turkey had not brought the seeds, they would have starved in the new world. No seeds. No food. No People.

First Woman spoke first. "Oh, my dear Turkey," she said gently, "You are not lazy or fat." She glared at Coyote. "You have saved us all. From now on, *your* feathers will be used in our prayer wands. You will be called "Rainmaker" because of the white foam Water Monster left on your tail."

And because Squirrel had thought to bring paint and brushes, the thirty-two clans and Animal and Bird People gathered around Turkey and decorated him with the colors of the seeds he had brought to the Fifth World. That is why Turkey is known as the Bird of Agriculture. And that is why he may always live near the homes of the First People and no one shall do him harm.

And so it remains to this day.

¤ ¤ ¤

ADAPTED FROM

Newcomb, Franc Johnson. "Turkey and the Big Reed." In *Navajo Folk Tales*, 23–41. Albuquerque: University of New Mexico Press, 1990.

Cougar, Wolf, Fox, and Bobcat

ROCK STARS: A STORY PECKED AND PAINTED ON STONE

LONG AGO, THE PEOPLE LIVED A HAPPY LIFE in a peaceful forest full of everything they needed.

But one dark day, a vicious tribe of tiny, aggressive people with teeny bows and poisoned arrows—who, by the way, were rumored to be man-eaters—invaded the homes of the People and drove them away.

What to do? Certainly there is little room for diplomacy when poisoned arrows and man-eating are part of the problem. The People turned for guidance to their healer and Keeper of Wisdom, Medicine Man. He had no clue what to do about these tiny, nasty people, so he announced to the People, "I will go on a vision quest and ask the animal spirits of our People for help." It had been a very long time since anyone had asked the animal spirits for help. Surely they would help their own kin, right?

He left at twilight and followed the bright evening star in the west toward the land of the animal spirits. He walked all night until dawn, when he came to a clearing in the forest, a meadow ringed with tall trees and high, scattered rocks carved with ancient stories pecked and painted on stone.

Standing in the middle of the clearing were the animal spirits of his People: Cougar, Wolf, Fox, and Bobcat. Cougar stepped forward: "It has been a very long time since you came to us. We thought you had forgotten our special kinship. Why are you here now?"

Medicine Man explained how the vicious little people had chased them from their homes, and that they did not know what to do. The animals listened carefully, and when Medicine Man finished, they gathered in Council to determine what was to be done. After some time, Cougar stepped forward and said to Medicine Man, "In honor of our ancient kinship, we

will help remove these vicious little people from your territory."

Gratitude flooded Medicine Man, as he offered his thanks to the animal spirits.

"But," Wolf added, "we have one condition."

"Anything!" Medicine Man responded.

"Your people and all your children to come must honor our ancient kinship with you and never again harm a cougar, wolf, fox, or bobcat," said Bobcat.

Medicine Man realized with shame that his People had forgotten their ancient kinship, and that hunters from his People had killed these very animals. Here was a chance to change that, to go back to honoring the old ways when the animals and People were as one family.

"You have my word," he said.

"That's nice," Cougar replied. "But we want the word of the People too. They are the ones killing our people. Go back and tell them the deal. If they agree, come back and we will help you."

So Medicine Man left, keeping the bright star in the west to his back now. When he arrived home, he called everyone to Council: the elders, warriors, women, and children. He told them what had happened and what the animal spirits would do for them.

Well, some of the warriors said of Medicine Man, "That crazy old fool—talking to a cougar. Let's just fight."

"He's leading us into a trap," said others.

But the elder ones remembered the stories from their grandmothers and grandfathers, of how the animals had once been kin to their People and were never harmed.

And a Keeper of Wisdom has the gift of sweet, powerful speech, so Medicine Man convinced the People that this was the only way. If they would follow him to the animal spirits and honor the deal to never harm them again, then all would be well.

The People followed him, some reluctantly (especially the warriors who always want a good fight). Others followed him, grateful for the chance that they might have peace again, while the elder ones followed him with joy that the old connection of kinship with the animals would be made new again.

They journeyed to the light of the bright star to the west, traveling all night. When at dawn they arrived at the clearing, they found Cougar, Wolf, Fox, and Bobcat standing next to the high scattered rocks of ancient stories pecked and painted on stone.

All the People as one fell to their knees in awe, even the grumpy warriors. And led by Medicine Man, the People proclaimed, "You are our kin. We will never harm you, Cougar, Wolf, Fox, and Bobcat. Nor will our children or children's children."

With the deal sealed, Cougar nodded to Wolf, Fox, and Bobcat, and they lifted Medicine Man into the sky. Suddenly, all around them were lightning bolts of fire raining down from Medicine Man to the forest, everywhere except the clearing where the People were gathered. The fire surrounded the vicious, cruel, little people with their tiny bows and poisoned arrows and turned them all to ash.

When Medicine Man was brought back to earth (with a look of amazement on his face), the fire was gone: the forest was calm and peaceful again.

"All is well now," said Cougar.

Medicine Man and the People thanked the animals, and Fox noted, "We didn't like those vicious little people anyway."

Medicine Man and the People returned to their home, and thanks to the renewed kinship with the animal spirits, lived a happy life in the peaceful forest. To this day, the People know not to harm their kin—cougar, wolf, fox, or bobcat—in honor of their promise to the animal spirits for making them safe and happy again.

And, if you happen to wander through the forest at twilight and stumble upon a meadow ringed with tall trees and high scattered rocks, there you will find, pecked and painted on stone, the story of the special enduring kinship between the People and Cougar, Wolf, Fox, and Bobcat.

¤ ¤ ¤

ADAPTED FROM

Campbell, Joseph. *The Way of the Animal Powers*. New York: Harper, 1988.

Clark, Ella, ed. "The Little People." *Algonquin Tribes: The Arapahoes, The Gros Ventres, and the Blackfeet*. In *Indian Legends from the Northern Rockies*, 232–235. Norman, OK: University of Oklahoma Press, 1966.

Clark, Ella, ed. "The Little People." *Shoshone Tribes: The Shoshones and the Bannocks*. In *Indian Legends from the Northern Rockies*, 180–182. Norman, OK: University of Oklahoma Press, 1966.

"The Wolf, the Fox, the Bobcat and the Cougar." *A Trip to the Moon*. Outdoor Idaho—Idaho Public Television. Last modified 2015. http://idahoptv.org/outdoors/shows/triptothemoon/wolffox.cfm.

Buffalo

UNDER REPAIR: THE GOOD RED ROAD

TWO YOUNG BROTHERS, ONE FOOLISH AND ONE WISE, were on the plains scouting game for their hungry people, when Buffalo Woman appeared out of the west, clad all in white and seeming to float on air.

"Whoa—you are smokin' hot!" leered the foolish young brother.

That is a bad pick-up line for a Holy Woman (or any woman for that matter). "So are you," Buffalo Woman replied, and fried him dead to the bone.

The wise and discerning brother knelt and said, "Oh, Holy One, what may I do for you?"

"Go tell your People that I bring a sacred message from the Buffalo People. Build me a medicine lodge, and in four days I will come," said Buffalo Woman.

Four days later, all was ready for her. The People anxiously scanned the west for her arrival, and Buffalo Woman finally appeared.

She carried a Sacred Pipe for the hungry People. "The wooden stem of the pipe," she said, "symbolizes all trees and plants. The red stone of the bowl represents the Buffalo People and your People. The smoke from the pipe embodies your prayers carried by the sacred wind to the Creator, Wakan Tanka," she explained.

"How do we use it?" the wise brother asked.

"Offer the smoke to the Sky and Earth, and to the four sacred directions. The smoke will bear to Wakan Tanka your understanding that everything on Earth is connected. If you remember this, then your prayers will always lead you in the right direction down the Good Red Road, the path of peace and harmony. Your People will be happy and well."

The People thanked Buffalo Woman, and then watched as she walked far to the west, rolled on the earth, and stood up as a black buffalo, a brown buffalo, a red buffalo, and finally a white buffalo. And then, as she disappeared over the horizon into the setting sun, just like that, buffalo appeared.

The People followed the Good Red Road and the directions Buffalo Woman gave them. Where the People were, so were the buffalo. They

hunted the buffalo with reverence and respect. Everything the People had came from the buffalo—their tipis, clothing, moccasins, containers, blankets, and the wisdom and understanding that everything on Earth is connected.

For many generations, the People and buffalo were happy and well.

Then the white people came.

Some were wise. Many were foolish.

The white men did not understand that everything on Earth is connected.

They did not follow the Good Red Road. The white men came to the sound of their own chant:

LAND land LAND land LAND land LAND land LAND land
Homestead, Railroad, Cattle, Fence
Land we want and Land we'll get
Nothing's ever stopped us yet.

The chant could be heard all over the People's land. It echoed in their tipis and dreams. It rippled through the tall prairie grass. It pulsed through the earth and sky and in all four sacred directions. It scattered the smoke of the Sacred Pipe into thin air.

Disharmony and discord fell upon the land and People.

The buffalo saw the hardship and suffering of the People they loved. They met in Council and agreed. "We must protect the People and the Good Red Road. We must fight the white man."

The buffalo tore up the railroad tracks. They chased the cattle. They knocked down the fences.

The white men fought back. Sporting men boarded trains and shot the buffalo out of the windows as they sped by. The army sent soldiers to kill their enemy. Yet the sporting men and soldiers could not defeat the buffalo.

But then, the army hired the buffalo hunters, men with one purpose: to kill the buffalo. They killed and killed and killed. They left the buffalo carcasses to waste and rot in the hot sun and tall prairie grass.

The buffalo skinners came. They piled high the bones and hides into wagons and took them to the railroad to ship east. It is said that the bones of the buffalo stretched for over a mile, stacked as tall as a man: a fence of death and devastation that severed the People from the Good Red Road.

There were too few buffalo left to fight. They had lost.

¤ ¤ ¤

One early misty morning, a young Sioux woman went to the spring for water. Out of the mist appeared an old buffalo cow, the ancient matriarch, followed by the few surviving buffalo. As the ancient buffalo cow walked toward the mountain with the last of her herd, the face of the mountain opened wide for them.

For a brief moment, the young woman glimpsed what was inside. Her breath caught and tears ran down her cheeks as she saw the wide green prairie of her childhood, a brilliant sun shining on the tall grasses. She heard a meadowlark singing and caught the scent of the blossoms on the plum tree. She saw the way the land had looked before the white men came. The way it would never look again.

She watched as the old buffalo cow walked into the mountain with the last of the Buffalo People.

The face of the mountain closed behind them.

The buffalo were gone.

¤ ¤ ¤

It is said that if Buffalo Woman appears again in the west, then the face of the mountain will open and the buffalo will return. The People will once again smoke the Sacred Pipe and walk the Good Red Road. They will be happy and well once more.

Or so it is said.

¤ ¤ ¤

ADAPTED FROM

Bruchac, Joseph. "The Passing of the Buffalo." In *Native American Animal Stories*, 99. Golden, CO: Fulcrum, 1992.

Bruchac, Joseph. "White Buffalo Calf Woman and the Sacred Pipe." In *Native American Stories*, 127–130. Golden, CO: Fulcrum, 1991.

Erdoes, Richard, and Alfonso Ortiz, eds. "The Buffalo Go." In *American Indian Myths and Legends*, 490–491. New York: Pantheon, 1984.

Riley, Jim and Dena. "Legend of the White Buffalo." *Native American Legends*. In *Legends of America*. Last modified March 2013. http://www.legendsofamerica.com/na-whitebuffalo.html.

Hummingbird

HUMMINGBIRD'S HEALING HARMONY

THE BIRDS ALL AGREED it was about time they had a decent physician.

"We need a Medicine Man to heal us when we are sick," said Oriole.

"Really, we need a good doctor around here," said Blue Jay disdainfully.

"Yes, we want someone who understands how to truly *heal*," said Thrush.

The birds gathered together in Council to decide the best candidate for Medicine Man. There was some argument back and forth, of course. The position of Medicine Man is held in the highest esteem by all the People. Plus, what parent wouldn't want their son or daughter to be a doctor?

But, ultimately, it came down to knowledge and background. Who had the most experience with flowers? Grasses? Herbs? Who knew best how to extract the pollen, nectar, honey, and healing juices from the People's extensive plant pharmacopeia?

The vote was unanimous: Hummingbird.

Sure, he was small—the birds called him Hosteen Yazzi, "Little Fellow," in the *Diné* tongue—but Hummingbird was also wise and heavily credentialed. He knew every single flower, herb, and grass in the area, and he spent his days sampling the nectar with his long, pointed bill.

Hummingbird was deeply humbled to be appointed Medicine Man (his folks were very proud and tried hard not to brag). Hummingbird was determined to take excellent care of the Bird People and immediately set about stocking his pharmacy. He extracted the juices and nectars of the plants to make his medicines and stocked up on acorn caps to mix them in. He stored everything in his home in the Big Cottonwood Tree.

It wasn't long before he had his first patient: Bluebird.

Bluebird arrived on a stretcher made of twigs and lined with soft cottonwood down, carried by Mockingbird, Oriole, Red-Winged Blackbird, and Warbler.

"Bluebird is too sick to fly!" cried Oriole.

The birds carefully set Bluebird down and looked on anxiously as Hummingbird fluttered over Bluebird and solemnly made his diagnosis: "Call all of our bird friends together. Tell them to meet at dawn to sing."

Mockingbird, Oriole, Red-Winged Blackbird, and Warbler immediately flew off in each of the four directions to share with the other birds the prescription from Hummingbird.

When dawn arrived, birds of every kind arrived at Hummingbird's Big Cottonwood Tree. They perched in a circle around Bluebird, who was sitting in a nest of twigs and down, and as the sun rose, they each sang their very own song as a prayer for their friend. (Since Mockingbird does not have his own song, he just borrowed from his friends; no one minded one bit.)

While the birds were singing their prayers, Hummingbird sat next to Bluebird in the middle of the circle with thirty-two acorn caps of medicine arrayed carefully in front of him. As he hummed his own song, he alternated between giving Bluebird a drink from an acorn cap, and then sprinkling pollen from the sacred red flower over her.

For three days Bluebird's friends gathered at dawn to sing for her, and each day Hummingbird repeated the treatment with the medicines in the acorn caps and the sprinkling of pollen from the sacred red flower. Then, on the fourth day, as the rays of the sun peeked over the mountains to the east, Bluebird hopped out of her little nest and sang out to all her friends: "I am well again!"

The birds were overjoyed that Bluebird was cured, and a symphony of jubilant song broke out to celebrate the good news.

The birds gathered around Hummingbird and congratulated him. "You are an excellent Medicine Man," they said, while his proud parents told anyone who would listen, "That's our son!"

Hummingbird bowed his head, iridescent in the morning sunlight, and whispered gratefully to each of the four sacred directions, "Thank you."

And so, whenever any of the birds were sick, they called on Hummingbird to heal them. Hummingbird's healing ways became so renowned that he even shared them with the Medicine Men of the Diné People, and for a very, very long time, those People, too, could be healed through the prayer and song of Hummingbird.

Now, none of the Diné People remember Hummingbird's healing song. Only Hummingbird remembers, but no one knows how to ask him anymore. Yet at dawn every day, the People pause and listen to the birds singing the healing songs to their sick friends, hoping to catch an echo of Hummingbird's prayer, and perhaps to heal themselves as well.

¤ ¤ ¤

ADAPTED FROM

Hausman, Gerald. "Humming Bird, the Medicine Man." In *Sitting on the Blue-Eyed Bear: Navajo Myths and Legends*, 94–6. Westport, CT: Lawrence Hill, 1975.

ACKNOWLEDGMENTS

For the last twenty-five years, Jan Taylor and I have dreamed of creating a book together. You are holding this book in your hands thanks to Aaron Downey, Managing Editor of Rio Nuevo Publishers, who is kind, clever, thoughtful, funny, and an excellent editor. Thank you, Aaron, for making our dream come true.

I was lucky enough to study about animals in mythology and literature with Professor Paul Zolbrod, who is renowned for his scholarship in retelling the Navajo Creation story and bringing an elevated understanding of Native literary tradition to the forefront of serious study. Paul has been my mentor for many years now, and generously agreed to be a source of advice, information, and direction regarding appropriate use of Native material for this book. Paul, your decades of scholarship and generosity of spirit made this book possible. Thank you.

Writing about Native stories means considering the authentic material from Native storytellers, scholars, ethnographers, and other accounts and adapting the stories in a manner that respects a living, vibrant belief system that has been sustained as an oral tradition for centuries. So thanks must also go to all those who have recorded and retold Native stories from the original unknown authors and visionaries. It is with humility and respect that we express our gratitude to their dedication to keeping alive Native literary tradition. Their knowledge is clearly the superior, and I am responsible for any unintentional errors.

And finally, thank you to the wise animals of the Southwest, who continue to invoke wonder, humility, inspiration, and delight.

RAE ANN KUMELOS is of Greek and Scotch-Irish heritage, meaning myth is in her DNA. Rae Ann holds a PhD in Mythology and Masters degrees in Mythology and Literature. She is a college professor of Mythology in her home state of California. Her specialty is animals in myth, literature, and life, and she has written for a variety of publications, most often about her furred, feathered, and finned friends. Her *Voice of the Animal* radio show is broadcast on XM Satellite Radio. Visit Rae Ann at www.voiceoftheanimal.com.

JAN TAYLOR has been a professional painter for thirty-five years. Best known for her wildlife paintings, equine art, and pet portraiture, she grew up in the Colorado Rockies where she developed a love for nature and all creatures. After receiving her fine arts and illustration degree from Northern Arizona University and working as a cowgirl, Jan settled in Cave Creek, Arizona, where she never lacks inspiration thanks to her many amazing rescued animals. You can see more of Jan's art at www.jantaylorart.com.

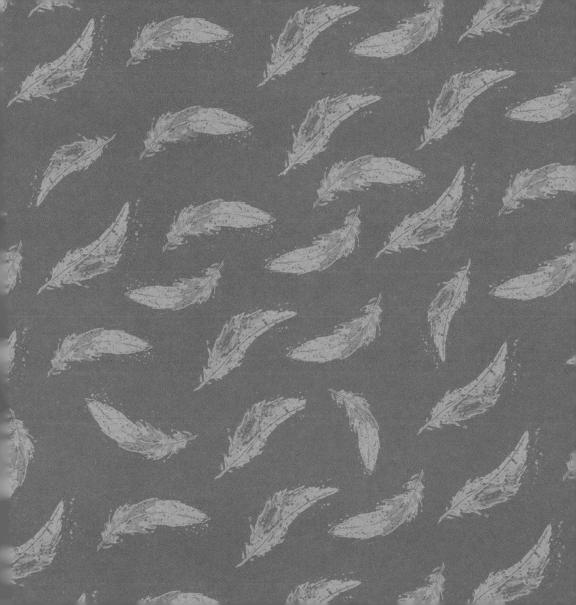

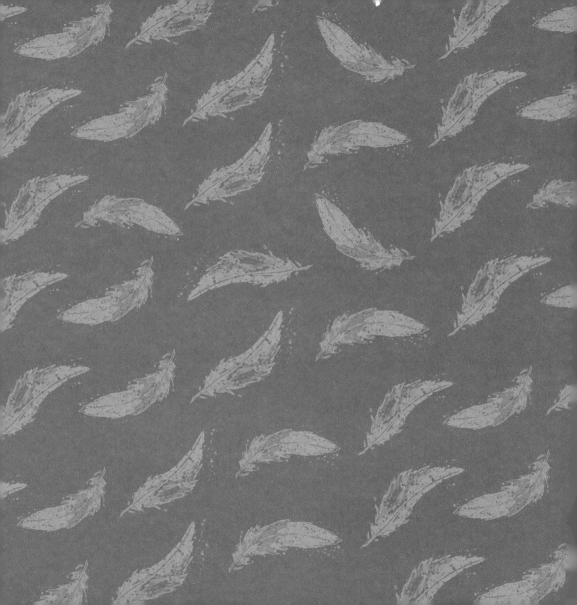